Children of the
Wild West

A frontier school

Children of the Wild West

RUSSELL FREEDMAN

CLARION BOOKS

TICKNOR & FIELDS: A HOUGHTON MIFFLIN COMPANY

NEW YORK

Quotation permissions and photographic sources are cited on page 97.

Clarion Books
Ticknor & Fields, a Houghton Mifflin Company

Printed in the U.S.A.

Library of Congress Cataloging in Publication Data
Freedman, Russell.
Children of the Wild West
Summary: Historical photographs with explanatory text
present a picture of life in the American West from 1840
to the early 1900s.
1. Children — West (U.S.) — Juvenile literature.
2. West (U.S.) — Social life and customs — Juvenile
literature.   [1. West (U.S.) — Social life and customs.
2. West (U.S.) — History — 1848–1950.   3. Photography of
children]   I. Title.
HQ792.U5F74   1983   305.2'3'0978   83-5133
ISBN 0-89919-143-6

P 10 9 8 7 6 5 4 3 2 1

Endpaper photo: School children in Central City, Colorado.
Courtesy Denver Public Library, Western History Division.

For my father

Contents

Frontier Photographers

ON MAY 19, 1841, a dozen covered wagons and seventy men, women, and children left Missouri and headed for the Pacific Coast. They were the first pioneers to travel west by wagon train. It is doubtful that any of these people had ever seen a photograph.

Photography was a new invention. The earliest photographs had been displayed for the first time in France just two years before, in the summer of 1839.

The growth of photography and the opening of the American West took place at the same time. By the 1850s, frontier photographers were traveling throughout the West. Their cameras were big and bulky. Their equipment was often crude. Even so, they were able to picture the frontier as the pioneers actually saw it.

In those days, simple rolls of film were unknown. Instead, photographers used large glass plate negatives that were messy and hard to handle. Just before a picture was taken, the glass plate was coated with sticky chemicals. It had to be placed in the camera and exposed right away, while it was still moist. Then the plate had to be removed from the camera and developed on the spot, before the chemicals dried. A photographer's covered wagon served as his darkroom. Wherever he went, he had to haul with him hundreds of pounds of photographic equipment.

The first cameras could not capture motion. Because of the long exposure time needed, the camera had to be placed securely on a tripod. The people being photographed had to stand or sit absolutely still. If anyone moved, the picture would be blurred.

A frontier photographer might take more than an hour to assemble a group for a portrait, prepare the glass negative, take the picture, and then develop the negative. Yet people were eager to pose in front of the camera. Some of them would have their picture taken only once in their lives.

By the 1880s, many advances in photography had been made. Cameras were becoming smaller and easier to handle. Faster shutters and shorter exposure times made action shots possible. Photographers no longer had to carry their darkrooms with them. They now used improved glass negatives that could be developed long after the picture was taken.

Hundreds of thousands of photographs were taken while the West was being settled. Over the years, a large number of these pictures were lost or accidentally destroyed. Others remained hidden away in forgotten family albums, in attics and store-rooms. But as time passed, the old photographs were discovered and placed in the archives of libraries, museums, and historical societies. Many of the photos that survive today are faded, scratched, or torn. But others, printed from undamaged glass negatives, are as clear and luminous as any photographs ever taken.

The photographs in this book give us a glimpse of the youngsters who traveled west with wagon trains and helped settle the frontier with their families. Through the eye of the camera, we can still see these children from a century ago, when they were growing up in the Wild West.

Posing for a frontier photographer

A wagon train drawn by teams of oxen. Near the center of the photograph, a woman cooks over an open fire.

Going West

IT WAS A TYPICAL wagon train of the 1840s. The swaying wagons, plodding animals, and walking people stretched out along the trail for almost a mile.

Near the end of the train, a boy holding a hickory stick moved slowly through the dust. He used the stick to poke and prod the cows that trudged beside him, mooing and complaining.

"Get along!" he shouted. "Hey! Hey! Get along!"

Dust floated in the air. It clogged the boy's nose, parched his throat, and coated his face. His cheeks were smeared where he had brushed away the big mosquitoes that buzzed about everywhere.

Up ahead, his family's wagon bounced down the trail. He could hear the *crack* of his father's whip above the heads of the oxen that pulled the wagon. The animals coughed and snorted. The chains on their yokes rattled with every step they took.

His mother sat in the front seat of the wagon, holding the baby on her lap. His sisters had gone off with some other girls to hunt for wild herbs along the road.

The family was traveling west along the Oregon Trail in what someday would be the state of Wyoming. They followed the sandy banks of the North Platte River past rocky hills dotted with sagebrush and greasewood. This was Indian country, the land of the Oglala Sioux.

Back in Missouri, their wagon had been a brand-new prairie schooner with red wheels, a blue body, and a fresh white canvas top. Now the top was stained and patched, the paint faded and crusted with mud. The wagon creaked and groaned, but it was still sturdy. On this hot July afternoon, the canvas cover had been rolled back and bunched so that any breezes could blow through the wagon.

The wagon was crammed with the family's possessions — with food, clothing, and furniture; with tools, bedding, kitchenware, and tent supplies. Tied to its side were a plow and a hoe. Hanging from a rope was a sealed pail of milk that bounced steadily as the wagon jolted along. By evening, the milk would be churned into butter.

There were forty wagons in the party, and nearly two hundred men, women, and children. A few of the pioneers rode saddle horses, but most of them walked. The only ones riding inside the wagons were little children with their mothers, and people who were sick or injured. Following the wagons were herds of milk cows and beef cattle, along with extra oxen, mules, and horses.

The pioneers had been up since four that morning, when the sentries started the day by firing their rifles. Hurrying about in the darkness, they had kindled fires, put on kettles of water, milked cows, pulled down tents, loaded wagons, and fixed breakfast. By seven, they were ready to roll. The train captain gave the signal to move out. Slowly the lead wagons rolled forward, and the others fell into line.

At noon they stopped for an hour's rest. The teams of oxen and mules were turned loose from the wagons but were not unyoked. Blankets and buffalo robes were spread out beside the trail. The pioneers ate a cold lunch, relaxed a bit, then rolled down the trail again.

As they moved along, they passed the splintered wreck of an abandoned wagon. Every two or three miles, they saw wooden grave markers where pioneers had been laid to rest beside the

Resting along the trail

trail. As the day wore on, children began to climb aboard the wagons, finding nooks and corners where they could curl up and nap.

Late that afternoon, near a grove of willows, the train captain gave the signal to stop for the night. One after another, the wagons pulled off the trail and began to form a large circle, or corral. The wagons were locked together, front to rear, with chains; the front tongue of one wagon reached under the rear wheels of the next. A gateway was left open to admit the livestock. Then the last wagon was rolled into place, sealing the corral.

Safely inside, the pioneers tended their cattle, pitched tents, and started campfires for the evening meal. Families sat together eating beans, dried buffalo meat, and camp-baked bread from tin plates.

By 8 P.M., sentries had taken their posts around the corral. Children ran past playing tag. Some girls sat in a circle, sharing secrets and laughing. A boy lay sprawled on his belly beside a campfire, studying a tattered copy of the *Emigrants Guide to Oregon and California*. Grown-ups stood in small groups, chatting and planning the day ahead.

Gradually the pioneers drifted off to their tents and wagons, where they huddled under blankets and fell asleep. Even in July, the night was chilly at this high altitude. They had traveled perhaps fifteen miles that day, nearly seven hundred miles since leaving Missouri in May. They still had more than twice that distance to go.

The first pioneers to travel west by wagon train had set out from Missouri in the spring of 1841. Each year after that, emigrants

An emigrant family poses for the camera in a tent attached to their wagon.

streamed westward in ever-increasing numbers. By 1869, when the first transcontinental railroad was completed, more than 350,000 pioneers had followed the ruts of the Oregon Trail across the continent.

At the beginning, most of them headed for the Pacific Coast. They went west to claim free land in the Oregon and California territories, to strike it rich by mining gold and silver, to settle in a new country where there was plenty of elbowroom and boundless opportunity.

They called themselves "emigrants" because, as they started their journey, they were actually leaving America. During the early 1840s, the United States ended at the banks of the Missouri River. The region that later would be Kansas and Nebraska had been set aside by the United States government as Indian territory. California was still a northern province of Mexico. The vast wilderness of the Oregon country was claimed jointly by the United States and Great Britain. Gradually these western territories would become part of the United States. But when the first emigrants set out, they were entering a foreign land.

Their journey started in one of the raw frontier towns along the Missouri River known as the "jumping-off places." Wagons rumbled through the muddy streets of these towns. Fur trappers and Indians mingled with westbound emigrants on sagging wooden sidewalks. Each year the wagon trains started rolling in late April or early May. Timing was crucial. If the emigrants started too early, they might not find enough spring grass on the prairie to graze their livestock. If they started too late, they might be stranded in the western mountains by early winter blizzards.

Several trails led west. The best-known and most popular by far was the Oregon Trail. It led across the Great Plains, climbed over the Rockies, then branched off toward Oregon in one direction and California in the other.

For most of its route, the Oregon Trail was little more than a pair of wheel ruts cutting across 2,400 miles of prairie sod, mountain rocks, and desert sand. When the trail came to a river, the ruts stopped at the water's edge. If the river was not too deep, the emigrants could ford it with their wagons. Otherwise they had to lift the wagons off their wheels and float them across on rafts, as their horses and cattle swam alongside.

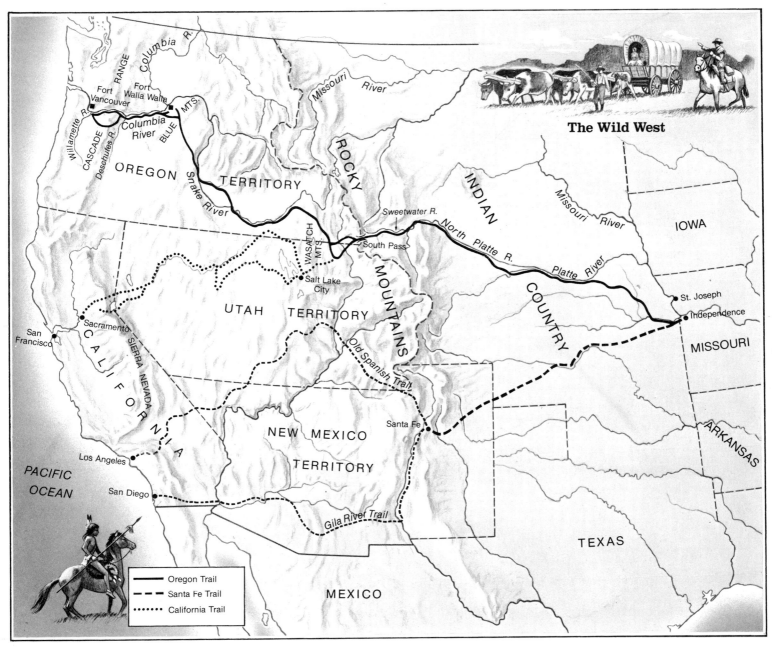

The Wild West

Map by George Buctel

Oregon Trail
Santa Fe Trail
California Trail

PACIFIC OCEAN

CALIFORNIA
San Francisco
Sacramento
Los Angeles
San Diego
SIERRA NEVADA

OREGON TERRITORY
Fort Vancouver
Fort Walla Walla
Columbia River
CASCADE RANGE
BLUE MTS.
Snake River
Willamette R.
Deschutes R.
Columbia R.

UTAH TERRITORY
Salt Lake City
WASATCH MTS.
South Pass

NEW MEXICO TERRITORY
Santa Fe
Old Spanish Trail
Gila River Trail

ROCKY MOUNTAINS

INDIAN COUNTRY
Sweetwater R.
North Platte R.
Platte River
Missouri River

IOWA
MISSOURI
St. Joseph
Independence

ARKANSAS
TEXAS
MEXICO

Fording a river

The first weeks on the trail were always the easiest. Their wagons were packed with fresh supplies; their animals were sleek and healthy. The land was flat, the weather often mild. The rippling grass of the Kansas prairie was sprinkled with wildflowers, and hummingbirds shimmered above fields of clover.

The emigrants enjoyed balmy days along the trail, but when they were caught in prairie storms, then they were miserable. Violent rainstorms came suddenly. Driving sheets of rain drilled against the canvas tops of wagons and tents and rose in a spray from the ground. Campfires fizzled out. Cooking was impossible. At times, top-heavy wagons were blown over and tents were uprooted by screaming prairie winds. Lightning flashed across the sky, and with the *crack* of thunder, the livestock sometimes broke away in terror. Riders had to gallop out and round them up. They came back drenched.

As the emigrants entered the foothills of the Rockies, the trail began to climb steadily uphill. Oxen and mules struggled against their loads. Teamsters shouted and cursed and lashed their whips to urge on their tired teams. To lighten the load, the emigrants began to dump cherished household possessions. Massive oak bureaus and mahogany claw-foot tables were left beside the road to crack and scorch under the western sun.

By now, hardship and fatigue showed in the emigrants' faces. At times it seemed that half of them were ill. Adults and children bounced along in wagons, burning with high temperatures or shivering with chills.

Gradually the trail climbed the Rockies. It crossed the continental divide at South Pass, a windy upland valley that cut through the mountains. Beyond the Rockies, the trail branched off. One branch led northwest toward the coast of Oregon. The other veered southwest toward California. At this point the emigrants were only about halfway to their destinations.

Emigrants bound for California had to cross the treacherous deserts of Utah and Nevada, then pull their wagons over the rugged Sierra Nevada. If they kept on schedule, they could make it across the mountains before the first winter snowfall. The road to Oregon followed the twisting Snake River along steep, boulder-strewn ledges. It passed through a desolate plateau, then climbed west over the Blue Mountains and the Cascades.

As the emigrants pressed forward, oxen and mules were overcome by heat and exhaustion. Animals stumbled in their tracks and dropped dead in the yoke. Their bleached bones became a common sight along the trail. Once past the deserts, wagons had to be hoisted up steep mountain slopes with chains and pulleys

Mormon emigrants crossing the Wasatch Mountains in Utah

and ropes, then eased down with their wheels locked. Sometimes chains snapped and wagons broke loose, careening down hills and toppling over mountain ledges.

If food supplies ran low, the emigrants had to slaughter their oxen and mules and eat them. Some pioneers were forced to abandon their wagons altogether and cross the mountains on horseback or on foot.

Babies were born during the westward journey, and many emigrants died. Some were killed in skirmishes with Indians, but that did not happen often. Accidents and disease killed far more emigrants than the Indians did. Epidemics of cholera and typhoid swept through wagon trains. People drowned during river crossings in plain sight of their families and friends. Children were bitten by snakes and caught in stampedes. They fell out of wagons and under the wheels or the oxen's hooves. One out of every seventeen emigrants who started the trip was buried beside the Oregon Trail.

Many emigrants spent six to eight months on the trail. Often it was November or December before they finally came down from the mountains into the fertile valleys of Oregon and California.

The end of the trail. These emigrants arrived in Baker City, Oregon, with a wagon pulled by a horse, a mule, two oxen, and a cow.

A frontier homestead

Settling Down

MARTHA ANN MORRISON was a thirteen-year-old Missouri farm girl when she traveled west with a wagon train in 1844. Her father had decided to pull up stakes and move his family to Oregon. He had heard glowing reports about the Willamette valley, where a pioneer could claim a square mile of free land by clearing the trees and building a cabin.

Years later, Martha recalled the hardships and adventures of their overland journey. "We did not know the dangers we were going through. The idea of my father was to get on the coast: no other place suited him, and he went right ahead until he got there."

Farmer Morrison and his family set out from Weston, Missouri, in May, 1844. Emigration to the West had started only three years before. As yet, there was no practical wagon route over the rugged mountains of western Oregon. When the Morrisons reached Fort Walla Walla, they abandoned their wagons, built large wooden rafts, and piled their possessions aboard. Then they floated down the mighty Columbia River through gales, snowstorms, and surging rapids.

They reached the Willamette valley at the height of the rainy season, on December 30, 1844. But their journey was not quite over. Farmer Morrison wanted to settle on the Clatsop Plains, near the mouth of the Columbia.

"We did not get there until the middle of January or the first of February," Martha remembered. "We went down the river Deschutes in an open canoe, including all the children; and when we got down, there was no way to get to the place where my father had determined to locate us, but to wade through the tremendous swamps. I knew some of the young men that were along laughed at us girls, my oldest sister and me, for holding up what dresses we had to keep from miring; but we did not think it was funny. We finally waded through and got all our goods. Mother was a very fleshy woman, and it was a terrible job for her to get through."

Like many pioneer girls, Martha married young. In the summer of 1846, a year and a half after reaching Oregon, she became the wife of John Minto, a hired hand who had helped drive her father's wagons across the continent. Martha was fifteen; John was twenty-four.

Oregon was still an untamed wilderness of prairie and timberland, with just a few frontier settlements. Most pioneers spent their first winter clearing a homesite and building a log cabin. They picked out the tallest, straightest trees, chopped the lumber into logs, and hauled them to the homesite. The logs were notched at each end. Then they were lifted into place, one atop another. Cracks in the rough cabin walls were plastered with small sticks and chunks of mud.

Once the walls were up, the cabin was roofed over with a frame of rafters, topped with timbers or with bark shingles. The floor was the bare earth. The fireplace was built of stones, the chimney of sticks plastered together with clay. Openings were cut out of the walls for windows and a door. At first, the windows were covered by sliding wood panels. Later, the pioneers added the luxury of glass windows and put in wooden flooring made from split logs.

Two pioneer boys outside their family's log cabin in Oregon

A pioneer family at the doorway of their Oregon cabin. The baby sleeps in a cradle made from a split packing crate. A birdcage hangs in the window.

Inside the one-room cabin, they built simple furnishings to replace the oak dressers and mahogany tables left beside the trail. Dining tables were made from split logs fastened together with wooden pegs. Beds were wooden platforms built into a cabin corner, with mattresses of moss or straw. Babies slept in cradles made from packing crates split in half. At night, the cabin was lighted by flames from the fireplace and by simple oil lamps.

During the 1840s, thousands of pioneers settled in the Oregon Territory. Lonely forests gave way to farms, dairies, and orchards. Flourishing towns began to dot the valleys, and steamboats puffed up and down the Willamette River, carrying goods, livestock, and people.

To the south, California was still a sleepy Mexican colony, with widely scattered cattle ranches and some tiny coastal settlements. In 1848, following the Mexican War, California became a territory of the United States. That same year, gold was discovered at Sutter's Creek near Sacramento. In 1849, the gold rush began in earnest as tens of thousands of pioneers surged into the new territory.

These early forty-niners were mostly young, single men. If they were married, they usually left their families in the East while they rushed to California to strike it rich. Some of the larger mining towns, like Sonora and Grass Valley, eventually attracted families. But most mining camps remained overwhelmingly male. Children were so unusual that tough, grizzled miners made a great fuss over them. Mark Twain told the story of a miner who gave a sack filled with gold dust for the privilege of kissing a new baby.

After a few years, the gold ran out and most of the mining towns declined. By then, however, California was the fastest-growing state in the Union. Emigrants continued to pour in, settling on farms and ranches and in the booming towns and

Citizens of Sierraville, a California mining town

cities. San Francisco grew from 800 people in 1848, the year gold was discovered, to more than 50,000 by 1855.

So far, the rest of the West remained largely unsettled. As emigrants rolled across the continent, they did not really think of settling on the Great Plains. Children's geography books of the time called this vast region the "Great American Desert." It lacked trees, water was scarce, the climate was harsh, and the wind seemed to blow constantly. The emigrants simply passed through on their way to the Coast, leaving the land to the Indians and the buffalo.

But then something unexpected happened. As the fertile valleys of the Far West filled up with settlers, newcomers took another look at the grassy plains. During the 1850s, treaties with the Indians opened much of this region to white ownership. In 1862,

Congress passed the Homestead Act, which allowed a settler to claim 160 acres of public land by living on it for five years.

At first, pioneers began to settle along the well-timbered rivers of eastern Kansas, Nebraska, and Minnesota. Later they spread out across the prairie, moving gradually into the uplands of Colorado, Wyoming, and the Dakotas. Many of them were immigrants from the countries of northern Europe, lured to the American West by the promise of free land. And when the Civil War ended in 1865, thousands of black pioneers, freed from slavery, joined the trek westward to claim land of their own.

On the treeless plains, the pioneers became known as "sod-busters." The prairie soil, called sod, was knitted together by thickly matted grass roots. It was so tough, it could not be cut with an ordinary plow. Since there was little timber available, most settlers had to build their homes with the only material available — chunks of sod cut from the soil with special plows.

Some families began their new lives in simple dugouts, carved out of a hillside with an ax, a shovel, and a pick. Often the builder would enlarge the dugout by adding walls and a roof made of sod bricks. A dugout was dark and cramped. It was hard to keep clean, since dirt from the roof and walls sifted into everything. But it was quick and easy to build. It provided a temporary home until the settlers could put up a more comfortable sod house.

When a sod house went up, blocks of sod weighing fifty pounds each were loaded into the family wagon and hauled to the building site. The blocks were stacked one atop another, with the grass side down, and were staggered like bricks. Cracks and crevices

A dugout home carved into a prairie hillside. The wagon above the dugout holds a load of sod to repair the roof.

were filled with loose dirt and mud, and spaces were left for windows and a door. The roof was a frame of crisscrossed willow or cottonwood poles, topped with brush and grass, and covered over with a final layer of sod.

Inside the house, the walls might be plastered with a mixture of lime and sand. The floor was usually the prairie itself. It took a full acre of sod to build a typical one-room house, which measured sixteen by twenty feet and weighed about ninety tons.

A sod house on the prairie

With its thick earthen walls, a tightly built sod house was snug and warm in the winter and as cool as a cave during the summer. Since it was fireproof, it offered protection against wind-driven prairie grass fires and flaming Indian arrows. But at times, it was damp and musty inside. During heavy rains, water seeped through the roof and dripped down on the settlers and their furnishings. Even in good weather, particles of dirt would drift down from the roof. Cheesecloth was tacked to the rafters to catch the falling debris. Wildlife was another problem. Field mice often tunneled through the walls, followed by snakes.

In time, these sod houses were transformed into cozy family homes. Dirt floors were covered with carpets, cowhides, or buffalo skins. The rough walls might be decorated with strips of bright gingham. Patchwork quilts covered the beds, and pots of flowers and herbs stood on the deep windowsills. Many families came to love their soddies — so much so that people continued to live in sod houses long after imported lumber was available for frame houses.

Wherever pioneers settled in the West, frontier towns began to appear. New gold and silver strikes in Oregon, Washington, Nevada, Idaho, and Colorado created dozens of booming mining

Former slaves on their Nebraska homestead

The main street of Granite, Oklahoma

towns. Ranchers drove herds of cattle across the plains to boisterous cow towns like Dodge City, where the animals were loaded into railroad boxcars and shipped east. Most of the new towns, however, were farming communities where homesteaders could sell their crops and buy supplies. Many pioneer families could drive their wagons into town, spend the day, and get home before dark.

A typical frontier town boasted a main street as wide as a field, allowing plenty of room for teams and wagons to turn around. It had raised wooden sidewalks, lined with hitching posts, which helped keep the pioneers' feet above the mud and dust of the street.

Every town had a livery stable and a blacksmith's shop. There was always a general store crammed with merchandise ranging from pickles to plows. Grown-ups gossiped around the store's

Shops in Manhattan, Kansas

potbellied stove, while children stood by the counter and eyed big glass jars filled with peppermint balls and striped candy sticks. As the towns grew, they offered more specialized shops like meat markets, drugstores, bookshops, and even ice-cream parlors.

A few western towns grew quickly into full-fledged cities. Salt Lake City, founded in 1847 as the center of the Mormon religion, became a prosperous manufacturing center with busy factories, an impressive theater, and a gigantic Mormon temple at the heart of the city. Denver, which started as a rough mining camp in 1858, ranked twenty years later as the richest community between Saint Louis and the West Coast. The biggest city in the West, and the most cosmopolitan, was San Francisco. Its harbor was jammed with ships from all over the world, its streets thronged with people speaking many languages.

When San Francisco's first public school opened in 1850, it had an enrollment of 148 pupils between the ages of four and sixteen. Only two of them had been born in California, and one in Oregon. The others came from seventeen eastern states and from ten foreign countries.

San Francisco's Chinatown

A Cheyenne encampment on the Great Plains

A Bannock family camped near Medicine Lodge Creek, Idaho

The American Indians

THE OREGON TRAIL cut straight through the heart of the Indian country. When the first wagon trains set out in 1841, most of the land west of the Mississippi River was occupied by Indian tribes.

Hundreds of tribes and bands were scattered through the western territories. Some tribes had lived in the West for thousands of years. Others had arrived only recently from the East. Pushed from their native lands by white settlers, they had been forced to pack up and move across the Mississippi.

These tribes differed greatly among themselves. They spoke different languages, observed different customs, and had different life-styles. The Cheyenne were free-roaming hunters and warriors who followed herds of buffalo across the plains. When they were on the move, they carried their homes with them, living in tipis made of buffalo skin. The Pueblo of the Southwest were settled farmers who lived in large adobe apartment houses and raised corn, cotton, and turkeys. The Chinook of the Northwest were expert fishermen, skilled with canoes. Their houses were built of wood.

At first, most Indian tribes were friendly to the pioneers who began to settle in the West. As wagon trains crossed the continent, Indians often acted as guides. They ferried emigrants across rivers and traded with them along the way. A few tribes were hostile to the newcomers, but to begin with, there was little trouble. All along the trail, meetings between Indians and the emigrants were usually peaceful.

In some regions, Indian children began to attend schools run by Christian missionaries. Some white children had Indian playmates and learned to carry on conversations in tribal dialects.

For the most part, however, the Indians and the whites lived in separate worlds. Indians visited frontier trading posts and towns, but white settlers rarely ventured into an Indian village. Most whites remained ignorant of the Indians' ways. They knew little about these native Americans whose language, dress, and customs were so different from their own.

Anyone who visited an Indian village would see children playing many familiar games. Indian youngsters walked on stilts, rode wooden stick horses, spun tops made of acorns, and tossed leather balls stuffed with animal hair. They enjoyed blindman's buff, cat's cradle, and hunt the button. They competed in one-legged hopping races, breath-holding contests, wrestling matches, and Indian versions of football and field hockey.

An adobe apartment complex in Taos, New Mexico

A Zuni family on the terrace of their adobe apartment

Little girls played house with deerskin dolls, putting them to bed in toy tipis or small willow lodges. They dressed up their pet puppies and carried them on their backs, like babies. Small boys set out on make-believe hunts and raids, armed with miniature bows and arrows. Sometimes they caught frogs or killed chipmunks and rabbits. Occasionally they came up against bigger game.

A Sioux tribesman named Ohiyesa recalled his boyhood adventure with a huge moose. He was playing by the shore of a lake with some other boys when they saw the moose swimming toward them.

"We disappeared in an instant, like young prairie chickens, in the long grass. I was not more than eight years old, yet I tested the strength of my bow string and adjusted my sharpest and best arrow for immediate service. My heart leaped violently as the homely but imposing animal neared the shore. . . .

"'Still,' I thought, 'I shall claim to be the smallest boy whose arrow was ever carried away by a moose.' That was enough. I gathered myself into a bunch, all ready to spring. As the long-legged beast pulled himself dripping out of the water and shook off the drops from his long hair, I sprang to my feet. I felt some of the water in my face! I gave him my sharpest arrow with all the force I could master, right among the floating ribs. Then I uttered my war whoop.

"The moose did not seem to mind the miniature weapon, but he was very much frightened by our shrill yelling. He took to his long legs, and in a minute was out of sight."

Youngsters of all ages rode ponies and horses. When children

A Kiowa boy on horseback

were only two or three years old, they were placed on a gentle horse and tied in the saddle. By the time a boy was five or six, he might have his own pony, a gift from his father or grandfather. He was already a good rider and was able to help herd the horses.

Older boys competed in races and riding contests. They showed off their skill by hanging on the side of a galloping horse, then swinging down to scoop up an object from the ground.

Sioux boys played a rough-and-tumble game called "throw them off their horses." The boys would choose up sides, mount their steeds, and charge. As their horses reared and neighed, they tried to wrestle each other down to the ground. If a boy lost his grip and fell off his horse, he was counted "dead." He was out of the game.

Children learned the skills and customs of their tribe from their parents, grandparents, aunts, and uncles. Boys were instructed in

A Navajo family working at a blanket loom. The five-year-old girl in the foreground is carding wool.

the arts of hunting, trapping, and fishing, in boatbuilding and horsemanship. They were taught how to make drums and war bonnets, shields and spears, bows and arrows. When a boy entered his teens, he went along on his first serious hunt. If he made a kill, he was highly praised. His father might celebrate the event by inviting other tribesmen to a great feast.

As a boy grew older, he began to accompany war parties on raids. At first he would help gather wood, hold the horses, and collect the enemy's arrows to be used against them. Gradually he learned to face danger and take his place as a man among the warriors.

Girls began to help their mothers when they were five or six. They learned to cook and sew, to create intricate beadwork and quillwork, to weave blankets, make baskets and pottery, fashion moccasins, decorate clothing, and tan buffalo hides.

Older girls looked after their baby brothers and sisters, carrying them about in softly padded cradleboards. Each tribe had its own style of cradleboard. A tiny dress made of shells or beads might hang near a baby girl's head, a little bow and arrow near a boy's.

"Life was softened by a great equality," a Sioux chief recalled. "All the tasks of women – cooking, caring for children, tanning, and sewing – were considered dignified and worthwhile. No work was looked upon as menial; consequently there were no menial workers."

Boys and girls alike were taught the traditional myths, rituals, songs, and dances of their tribe. They learned the names of the

Two Kiowa girls with a baby in a cradleboard

A sick Sia boy being treated by five medicine men

spirits that dwelt in the trees, rocks, streams, and hills bordering their lands, how to understand those spirits and ask for their help.

Children were scolded for lying, for quarreling, and for disrespect to old people. While most parents were strict, they rarely struck their children. Instead, they disciplined them with stern words and nasty looks. When children really got out of line, they were ridiculed and belittled. The worst punishment a child could receive was to be shamed in the eyes of the tribe.

As more and more settlers arrived in the West and claimed land, troubles arose. The land they claimed was usually Indian land. Indians began to suspect that the white man had come to take permanent control of their hunting grounds.

Most whites believed that it was the destiny of the United States to occupy and develop the entire continent from sea to sea, and to convert the Indians to the white man's own civilized ways. Some settlers regarded the "red man" as a primitive savage, a member of a lesser race who must be expelled from settled regions and packed off to reservations. Settlers were spreading rapidly across the frontier. They felt that the Indians had no right to stand in their way.

During the 1850s, Indian tribes were persuaded or forced to give up more and more of their territory. In return, the United States government signed hundreds of treaties setting aside reservations for the exclusive use of the tribes. The government also promised to pay the Indians for the loss of their lands. But often the treaties were ignored and the promises forgotten. Many Indians found themselves exiled to isolated reservations where they could no longer hunt and live freely as they had in the past. For them, life on the reservation meant poverty and despair.

All along, the Indians were being urged to give up their traditional ways, to exchange their bows and arrows for the white man's plow. On some reservations, the United States government offered to build brick houses if the Indians would agree to settle down and live as the white man said they should. Many Indians used the brick houses for storage and continued to live in their familiar tipis. Some began to wear the clothing of the white man. Others clung to their traditional Indian robes.

Indians were being urged to give up their traditional ways. This photograph was taken on the Santee Sioux reservation in Minnesota in 1862.

On the grassy plains, the hunting tribes had depended on buffalo for their livelihood. Buffalo supplied much of their food and nearly everything else they needed – leather for their tipis and clothing; fur for their rugs and blankets; bones for their cups and spoons, knives, and arrowheads. To the Plains Indians, the buffalo was a sacred animal. It was to be killed only as needed, to be worshiped before every hunt, to be praised and thanked for its many gifts.

White hunters did not regard the buffalo so highly. During the 1850s and 1860s, millions of the animals were slaughtered for meat and leather and often for sport. At the beginning of the 1800s, perhaps 60 million buffalo had roamed the continent. By 1850, at least 20 million remained. But by 1870, the American buffalo was nearly extinct.

Along with the loss of their buffalo, thousands of Indians lost their lives to new and terrible diseases they had not known before. Pioneers traveling west had carried with them epidemics of cholera, smallpox, and measles. The Indians had no natural immunity to these European diseases, so their death rate was high. Some tribes lost more than half of their members.

Meanwhile, frontier towns and homesteads were springing up everywhere. Pioneers were demanding that more Indian territory be opened to white settlement. Throughout the West, the Indians were being pushed aside by white farmers, miners, and cattlemen. Some tribes gave in peacefully. But others, feeling cheated and betrayed, vowed to resist. They began to fight for the land they regarded as theirs.

Skirmishes and battles erupted between angry tribesmen and United States Army troops. The army made surprise raids on Indian villages. The Indians attacked wagon trains, homesteads, and border settlements. While most settlers never experienced violence by the Indians, they did hear terrifying stories and rumors about Indians on the rampage. In some parts of the West, fearful pioneers slept with loaded rifles by their sides. Wagon trains hurried along the trails, watching for signs of trouble, never knowing if the Indians might attack.

By the 1860s, full-scale warfare had broken out. For years, Indians fought a guerrilla war against the white invaders, while army troops pursued the Indians and fought pitched battles with

A Kiowa boy   Two Comanche girls

them. The army battled the Apache in the Southwest, the Nez
Percé in the Northwest, the Sioux, Comanche, and Cheyenne on
the Great Plains. On both sides, there were raids and reprisals,
massacres, and atrocities.

"What do we have to live for?" asked an Indian chief. "The
white man has taken our country, killed all our game. Not satisfied

with that, he has killed our wives and children. Now no peace. We want to go and meet our families in the spirit land. We have raised the battle ax until death."

The fighting reached its peak between 1869 and 1875, when more than two hundred pitched battles were fought. While the Indians won some important battles, they had no real hope of ever regaining their lands. Outnumbered and poorly armed, wasted by warfare and disease, they were finally subdued. The last major battle of the Indian wars was the massacre at Wounded Knee Creek in South Dakota on December 29, 1890, when more than two hundred Sioux men, women, and children were shot down by army troops.

At one time, the Indians had held all the land in America. By 1890, they held only about 200,000 square miles. The rest of the land – about 3 million square miles – had been taken by the whites. Even then, the Indians did not enjoy the same rights as other Americans. It was 1924 before they were granted citizenship and voting rights.

As the Indian wars ended, the government made new efforts to change the ways of the Indians and bring them into the society of the whites. At schools on reservations, Indian youngsters were taught modern farming methods and practical trades. Many young Indians were sent to special boarding schools in the East, like the Carlisle Indian School in Pennsylvania. Founded in 1879, Carlisle was the first school of its kind to be established off a reservation. Its students came from nearly every tribe in the United States.

The purpose of Carlisle and similar schools was to train young Indians in "the ways of civilization." Richard H. Pratt, the founder

The Chiloco Indian Training School in Oklahoma

of Carlisle, believed that the Indians could flourish in Ameria only if they exchanged their own culture for that of the whites.

Some graduates of Indian schools went on to take their places in white society. But many others did not want to adopt the white man's version of civilization. They returned to their reservations, where they preferred to live, as much as possible, in the traditional ways of their ancestors.

In 1867, a Comanche chief named Ten Bears had expressed the feelings of his people: "I have heard that you intend to settle us on a reservation near the mountains. I don't want to settle there. I love to roam over the wide prairie, and when I do it, I feel happy and free. When we settle down, we grow pale and die.

"Hearken well to what I say. . . . A long time ago this land belonged to my fathers, but when I go up to the river I see a camp of soldiers, and they are cutting my wood down or killing my buffalo. I don't like that, and when I see it my heart feels like bursting with sorrow. I have spoken."

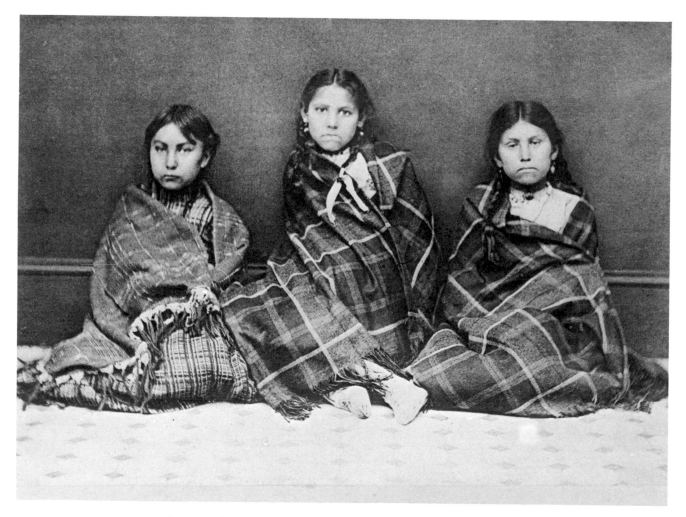

Three girls on their arrival at an Indian boarding school in 1878

The same girls fourteen months later

A group of boys on their arrival at an Indian boarding school in 1878

Some of the same boys fifteen months later

A sod schoolhouse

Frontier Schools

"I REMEMBER THE FIRST school I attended, a room crowded full of big boys and girls, noise and confusion, with now and then a howl from some boy that was being whipped. I and my brother, with another boy, occupied a bench with no back, near the stove. When the stove became too warm, we whirled around and faced the other side. The boy with us wore a paddle fastened around his neck. On this paddle were posted several letters of the alphabet and these were changed [by his parents] every day. How I envied that boy because his folks were making so much pains with him."

Those are the memories of Roxana Rice, a pioneer girl in Kansas. With its hard wooden benches and cast-iron stove, her one-room schoolhouse resembled thousands of others on the western frontier.

When settlers first moved into an area, there were no schools of any kind. Children were taught at home, or at the home of a neighbor. A pioneer woman would take time from her endless tasks to gather a circle of children around her and teach them reading, writing, and arithmetic. Lacking a blackboard, she used a long stick to scratch out letters and numbers on the dirt floor of the family cabin.

As soon as there were enough children in an area, families would band together to put up a proper school. Everyone contributed labor and materials for the schoolhouse, which often served as a church on Sundays.

The first schoolhouse was usually a simple cabin built of logs, sod, or adobe. Each morning students were called to class by the iron bell that hung outside the schoolhouse door. They came by foot, on horseback and in wagons, carrying their books, their slates and tablets, and their dinner pails. Some of them had to travel several miles in each direction.

Youngsters of all ages were taught by a single teacher. Schools, like frontier homes, sometimes had dirt floors. Since there was no running water, everyone drank from the same bucket and dipper kept in a corner of the room. The "playground" was the field outside. The "rest room" was an outhouse. Dogs of many breeds and sizes hung around the schoolhouse, whining at the door and sneaking inside to lay at their owners' feet.

Some early schools had no blackboards, no charts, maps or globes, no special equipment of any kind. Since textbooks were scarce, students brought whatever books they had at home. They arrived at school with an assortment of dictionaries, histories, encyclopedias, and storybooks. Many had copies of McGuffey's Readers, popular schoolbooks of the day that were filled with inspiring stories about hard work, honesty, and piety. Other students might have only a family Bible or an old almanac for their reading lessons.

The reading lesson

Much of the classroom time was devoted to the three Rs, along with American history and geography. Students memorized grammar rules, recited history dates, practiced penmanship and arithmetic tables, read aloud, and competed in spelling bees. Since the pupils might range in age from seven or eight to sixteen or older, they were not separated into grades. The teacher worked with one or two students at a time, while the others studied by themselves. Older students often tutored younger ones.

The youngsters attended classes only as their chores and the weather allowed. On an ordinary school day, many youngsters were up at 4 A.M., milking cows, chopping wood, toting water, and helping fix breakfast before leaving for school. After a full day of classes, they might do other chores by moonlight so as not to miss the next day's classes.

Since some children lived miles away from the nearest school, they might not attend classes at all until they were half grown. It was not uncommon to find youngsters twelve or fourteen years old who were just starting school for the first time. During the 1860s, fewer than half the youngsters in Oregon received any

Getting ready to board the school bus

formal schooling. California did not make education compulsory until 1874, when a law was passed requiring children between the ages of eight and fourteen to attend classes during at least two-thirds of the school year.

Many frontier schools found it difficult to find and keep good teachers. The pay was low. A teacher might earn anywhere from ten dollars to thirty-five dollars a month, paid only while school was in session. In some areas, the school year lasted only three or four months.

To help make up for the low pay, teachers often received free room and board. They lived with the families of their pupils,

This well-equipped classroom had a big cast-iron stove, and a real blackboard.

Lunchtime. An old tobacco tin and a lard pail serve as the girls' lunch boxes.

moving from one home to another, staying longest with families that had the most children in school. Since so many pioneer families lived in small crowded cabins, this system could be tough on the teacher.

Few teachers had any formal training. To receive a teaching certificate, they had only to pass simple examinations in basic subjects. Some schools were glad to accept almost anyone who was willing to take on the job.

Teachers were especially hard to find in California's mining camps. At a mining town in Tuolumne County, an unsuccessful gold-seeker named Prentice Mulford applied for a teaching job. He was examined by the school trustees – a doctor, a miner, and a saloonkeeper. "I expected a searching examination, and trembled," Mulford recalled. "It was years since I had seen a schoolbook. I knew that in geography I was rusty and in mathematics musty. Before the doctor lay one thin book. It turned out to be a spelling book."

Mulford was asked to spell *cat, hat, rat,* and *mat.* When he did this perfectly, the doctor told him, "Young man, you're hired."

Not all frontier schoolteachers could spell as perfectly as young Mulford. In 1859, the superintendent of schools in Sacramento, California, complained that some teachers were misspelling the name of the state they were teaching in as *Callifornia* or *Calafornia.*

Some teachers were barely older than their pupils. Often they hoped to learn as much as they taught. In 1855, Charles A. Murdock organized the first public school in Arcata, California:

"There was no school in the town when we came. It troubled my mother that my brother and sister must be without lessons. Several other small children also were deprived of the opportunity. In the emergency we cleaned out a room in the store . . . and I organized a very primary school.

A frontier classroom just before Christmas

"I was almost fifteen, but the children were good and manageable. I did not have very many, and fortunately I was not called upon to teach very long. There came to town a clever man, Robert Desty. He wanted to teach. There was no school building, but he built one all by his own hands. He suggested that I give up my school and become a pupil of his. I was very glad to do it. He was a good and ingenious teacher. I enjoyed his lessons about six months, and then I felt I must help my father."

Eventually school boards began to adopt rules that no teacher under sixteen years of age could be hired. As late as 1880, however, the United States Census reported that California still had one boy and two girl teachers under sixteen.

Discipline in the classroom was not usually a serious problem for female teachers. In those days, they were respected because they were women. A male teacher, however, might have to earn the respect of his older students. He might find himself confronted

The students and faculty of School District No. 32

Seven schoolboys ride a patient cow

with husky teenagers who had driven oxteams across the continent, fought Indians, mined gold, shot grizzlies, and may have just split a cord of wood before galloping off to class that morning.

These older boys had developed the habits of frontiersmen and were not used to the discipline of a classroom. Many of them had never attended a school before. On their first day of class, they would walk around the room, talk, whistle, and throw things. When they took their seats, fistfights broke out. A school superintendent in Santa Clara, California, demanded an end to "the use of tobacco amongst the grown boys, for the smell is quite disgusting to visitors on entering. Moreover, the constant expectoration [spitting] under the desks renders the room quite filthy."

Some teachers were not reluctant to use a rawhide whip. One of them reported that he had whipped thirteen boys the first day of class. Each day thereafter he whipped fewer boys, until finally he was able to put the whip away.

At Castroville, California, a young teacher named Tom Clay had no problems at all with discipline. The first day of class, he stood up, smiled at the students before him, and placed a six-shooter on his desk. "We're here to learn," he announced. "If anyone misbehaves, there's going to be trouble."

Gathering cow chips

Building the West

AT A FRONTIER SCHOOL in California, a boy was having trouble with his studies. His notebooks were a mess. His face was always smeared with ink. When he was called on to recite, his memory failed him. Years later his teacher, Prentice Mulford, recalled the student.

"He would hold a pen as he would a pitchfork. . . . He was not a regular scholar. He was sent to school only when it was an 'off-day' on his father's ranch. In the scholastic sense, he learned nothing.

"But that boy at the age of fifteen would drive his father's two-horse wagon, loaded with fruit and vegetables, 150 miles from California to Nevada over the rough mountain roads of the Sierras, sell the produce to the silver miners of Aurora and adjacent camps, and return safely home. He was obliged in places to camp out at night, cook for himself, look out for his stock, repair harness or wagon and keep an eye out for skulking Indians."

Scholars or not, frontier youngsters learned to take on responsibilities early in life. They began to help out around the homestead

Daily chores

as soon as they were old enough to follow instructions. A pioneer family needed all the help it could get.

Small children were expected to feed the chickens, gather the eggs, weed the vegetable garden, and pick wild nuts, berries, and fruits. As they grew older, they joined in the heavier work of plowing and planting, tending livestock, hauling water, pitching hay, building cabins and fences, hunting and trapping, cooking, washing, and cleaning.

As a rule, girls helped their mothers with the endless household

Baking sourdough biscuits

tasks, while boys labored in the fields with their fathers. When necessary, girls and their mothers did heavy farm work. Boys and their fathers washed clothes and learned their way around the kitchen.

Margaret Mitchell was an able-bodied girl on a Kansas homestead during the 1870s: "There were nine children in our family, six girls and three boys, and as the girls were older and my father not strong, the hard toil of the pioneer life fell to the lot of the girls. We used to set traps on the banks of the Republican and caught wolves, badgers, bobcats and skunks. Wild turkeys were very plentiful then, and we sometimes used traps to catch them.

"We had some very interesting and thrilling experiences with some of the animals we caught. One day an older sister and I were out looking at our traps and noticed that a big bobcat that was caught had climbed a tree with the chain hanging to him. I sat and watched him while my sister went for a gun and shot him. . . .

"Our house was made of logs, and the girls all helped with the construction of it. The cave we made ourselves and were justly proud of the work, for no one in our neighborhood had a better one."

An important chore on every homestead was hauling the family's daily water supply. Water had to be brought from a well, a spring, or the nearest creek, which might be a mile away. Big wooden buckets filled with water were hung at either end of a yoke. Balancing the yoke on his shoulders, a boy (or girl) would trudge back to the cabin with the buckets swinging and the water sloshing.

Another regular job was keeping the stove and fireplace supplied with fuel. Where there was enough timber, youngsters gathered and chopped firewood. On the treeless plains, they collected anything that might burn — twigs, grass and hay, sunflower stalks, dried corncobs. The most common fuel on the plains was buffalo or cow chips — chunks of dried manure left by the grazing herds. Children were sent out to gather this precious fuel in big baskets and wheelbarrows. The chips were carried home, stored in old gunnysacks, and tossed into the cookstove as needed.

The hay wagon

Children helped care for the barnyard animals. They fed and watered the livestock, milked the cows and goats, herded the hogs and sheep. Sometimes they made games out of their chores. One girl was put in charge of the family's hogs, with her little brother as a helper. They gave each hog a name. "I used to make my brother believe that they were talking when they grunted," she recalled. "I was able to understand their hog Latin and I would interpret to him."

Just about every western child learned to handle a horse. Youngsters on horseback drove cows to pasture and went galloping off on errands. Often a boy or girl would manage a two- to four-

A young cowboy

horse team pulling a wagon or plow. On cattle ranches, young-sters were sent on long rides to mend fences, inspect water holes, and search for lost calves. A British visitor to the frontier advised his countrymen back in England: "Learn to ride as soon as you possibly can. A man or boy who cannot ride is, in a new country, about as valuable as a clerk who cannot write in a city office."

Ordinary household chores took up a great deal of time on a pioneer homestead. Long hours were spent in the kitchen canning fruit, preserving meat, baking bread, roasting coffee beans, churning butter. Families made their own candles, their own soap, and their own home remedies. Children drank buttercup tea for asthma. They swallowed cough syrup made from onions mashed in sugar. When they had a fever, they were rubbed down with a salve of skunk grease mixed with turpentine.

Much of the pioneers' clothing also was made at home. On quiet evenings, girls sat by the fireside with their mothers, sewing skirts and trousers, knitting sweaters and socks, fashioning leather hats, coats, and shoes. They stitched window curtains, stuffed pillows, and embroidered linens. And they worked on handmade quilts that are so beautiful, some of them can be seen today in many museums.

Pioneer families often had a hard time raising cash between crops. To help out, children took jobs on neighboring homesteads or in nearby towns. Boys and girls alike were hired to pick fruit and harvest grain. Girls fresh from the classroom went to work as teachers in country schools. Boys worked as messengers and store clerks, as apprentices to blacksmiths, harness makers, and carpenters. They pushed wheelbarrows in brickyards, groomed horses in livery stables, swung axes in coal mines, and set type in the offices of local newspapers.

Some boys became full-time cowhands on cattle ranches while they were still in their teens. After the Civil War, many teenage cowboys were black youngsters who had learned the skills of roping and riding as slaves on Texas ranches. Many others were young Mexicans and Indians. Nearly one cowboy in three, of

Working in the fields

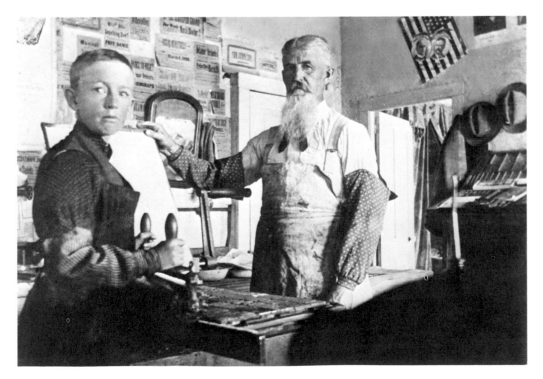

A young assistant in a newspaper office

California Special Messenger Service

any age, was either Mexican or black. One of the best known was Nat Love, born in a Tennessee slave cabin in 1854. At the age of fifteen, he rode into Dodge City and found work as a trail herder, driving beef cattle from Texas to Kansas. Later he became famous as a rodeo star.

Quite a few youngsters performed with the variety shows and circuses that journeyed constantly through the West. These young troupers usually traveled with their parents, who were also performers. Rowe's Circus featured Master Rafael, who won cheers from the crowd as his horse leapt through a flaming hoop. Lee's Circus starred Masters Eugene and Francis, sons of the owner, who were celebrated for their "incredible feats" on horseback. Marsh's Juvenile Comedians traveled from town to town with a

Young acrobats

troupe of twenty-six girls and four boys, ranging in age from five to fifteen.

The most popular child star on the western frontier was Lotta Crabtree, the daughter of an unlucky gold miner in Rabbit Creek, California. "We lived in a log cabin, my father, my mother, and I," Lotta recalled. "My father had been seeking gold, but he didn't have any success, and we were very poor."

Lotta had a sure sense of rhythm and a winning personality. She was taught some dances by Mart Taylor, a neighbor who owned one of the ramshackle little theaters found in every mining camp. Taylor persuaded Lotta's mother to let the child perform in one of his shows. She appeared on stage for the first time in 1855, when she was seven years old.

"I remember the night of my debut. The hall was full of miners. There were candles for footlights, and the room smelled strongly of tobacco smoke. I stepped bravely out. When I was through they roared applause, so much that I was terrified, and they threw to me nuggets of gold. That started my stage career. My mother received offers from other mining camps to let me appear. I learned to play the banjo and to sing the popular songs of the day."

With her sprightly singing, dancing, and reciting, Lotta became a hit in the mining country. She began to perform throughout the West, traveling from town to town with her mother, and playing with her dolls between performances. By the time she was nine, she headed her own company. She went on to become America's highest paid actress. When she died in 1924, she left an estate of $4 million — a lot more than any gold miner.

A children's band in Sonora, California

Games, Parties, and Celebrations

WHEN PIONEER CHILDREN finished their chores, they had the wide open spaces as their playground. They explored creek beds with their dogs, hiked to the top of sun-parched hills, raced across dusty fields on their ponies, and spent long summer days at the local swimming hole.

Sarah Bixby remembered her childhood summers on a California ranch during the 1870s: "We could go down to the orchard, where all summer long there were ripe apples and pears, or we could shed our shoes and wade in the San Gabriel. . . . We could watch hundreds of pigeons flying in and out of the deserted adobe ranch house, known to us, because of its condition, as 'The Flea House,' or we could go to our retreat in an enlarged coyote hole in the pasture on the other side of the hill. Luckily we did not find any rattlesnakes sharing it with us. We could play in the old stagecoach left in the weeds outside the fence. It remained from earlier days, when it carried the mails, express, and passengers between San Diego, Los Angeles and San Francisco."

On weekends and holidays, pioneer families relaxed at church

A birthday party at a Colorado ranch

socials, community dances, and neighborly house parties. They gathered for picnics in the churchyard, or in some shady grove beside a creek. Each family brought baskets and buckets heaped with food. Often they barbecued fresh pork or buffalo meat over open fires. After lunch, children jumped rope, played tag, and flew homemade kites. Everyone joined in songfests, ball games, and foot races.

Dancing was a favorite pastime among youngsters and grown-ups alike. At housewarmings, weddings, and holiday celebrations, settlers decked out in their Sunday best enjoyed round after round of polkas, waltzes, and square dances. Special community dances might be held almost anywhere — on a big outdoor platform, in the local schoolhouse or courthouse, in a livery stable that had been cleared and decorated for the occasion. Everyone went to these affairs — small children, young couples, parents, and grandparents. A local fiddler played the popular tunes of the day. Folks on the sidelines clapped their hands and tapped their feet as a caller led the dancers through their steps: "Swing an' march —

A lawn party in Orofino, Idaho

Getting ready for the Saturday night dance

first couple lead, clear round the hall and then stampede!"

Children always looked forward to spending a Saturday afternoon in town. The main street was crowded with suspendered men and sun-bonneted women from outlying homesteads, and with fancy visitors from the East. Cowboys wearing boots and spurs swaggered down the wooden sidewalks. Indians wrapped in blankets traded at the general store. At the stage depot, youngsters watched coaches swing out for some distant city and wondered if the passengers would make it safely to their destination. Sometimes a photographer passed through town, using his wagon as a studio. He would set up his big, boxlike camera and invite settlers to stand and pose as he captured the images we see today.

Nearly every frontier town was visited by the entertainers and variety shows that traveled back and forth through the West. Magicians, jugglers, snake charmers, and sword swallowers performed before coin-tossing crowds in the town square. No town was too small to attract the itinerant peddlers who carried suitcases filled with patent medicines. People would gather as the golden-voiced medicine man set up shop in some weed-grown empty lot. After bringing the crowd under his spell, he would unpack his miraculous wares: Hamlin's Wizard Oil, Dr. John Bull's Vegetable Worm Destroyer, Dr. B. P. Sherman's Pricklyrash Bitters. Sometimes he convinced his listeners that his medicines really worked, and always, he entertained them.

Most towns had a theater where professional troupes played one-night stands, performing everything from slapstick comedies to tear-jerking melodramas. Enthusiastic audiences shouted warnings, advice, and encouragement to the actors. Shakespeare's plays

Buying Too-Choos in town

were so popular in the West that many theatergoers knew the lines by heart and were not afraid to yell them out if an actor hesitated. Even small communities without professional theaters had amateur theatrical groups that performed in schoolhouses and town halls.

Every summer, at least one traveling circus would roll into town. Children flocked from miles around to watch the circus parade down the main street with its brass bands, tumbling clowns, prancing horses, marching elephants, whistling calliopes, and wagon after wagon of wild animals growling and roaring in their cages. Youngsters ran alongside and followed the parade to the outskirts of town, where they watched and sometimes helped the roustabouts put up the big tent and unload the animals. These

A circus parade marches down the main street of Salida, Colorado.

frontier circuses were not so different from the ones we have today. But in an age when movies and television were unknown, they had no competition as "The Greatest Show on Earth."

Another pleasure of a frontier childhood was the chance to celebrate an old-fashioned Christmas. If a family lived near a stand of evergreens, they would pick out a tree, chop it down and carry it home. The tree was decorated with strings of cranberries and popcorn, with colored ribbons, paper cutouts and candy apples. Candle holders cut from tin were fastened to the branches. Sometimes there were little wooden animals and people, drums and boxes, all of them carved and painted by hand.

On Christmas Eve, the smells of freshly made cakes, cookies, and candies drifted through the house. Long red stockings by the fireplace were stuffed with Christmas taffy and gingersnaps, and with gifts for each child. Friends and neighbors shared a festive holiday dinner. Afterwards they recited Christmas poems and prayers and sang traditional carols as the fireplace glowed and the candles flickered on the tree.

Christmas was a time for families and friends to celebrate at home. The Fourth of July was a community event, celebrated by the whole town. It was the one day of the year when everyone who could possibly make it headed for town to join the festivities:

A great 4th of July at Douglass, 1871, everybody is invited to come and bring filled baskets and buckets. There will be a prominent speaker present, who will tell of the big future in store for southern Kansas. Grand fireworks at night! Eighteen dollars worth of sky rockets and other

Christmas toys. Store-bought toys like these were a luxury on the frontier.
Most children received simple homemade gifts.

brilliant blazes will illuminate the night! There will also
be a bunch of Osage Indians and cowboys to help make
the program interesting. After the fireworks there will be
a big platform dance, with music by the Hatfield Brothers.

At sunrise on the Fourth, a cannon was fired in the town square. If the town had no cannon, gunpowder was exploded on a blacksmith's anvil. These salutes could be heard for miles. Children in outlying homesteads would get up before dawn and listen closely as the sounds of the explosions reached them, first from one direction, then from another.

When the morning chores were finished and an early breakfast gulped down, families packed their picnic baskets, hitched up their teams, and drove into town. Wagons and buggies were

A float in an Independence Day parade

A footrace at a Fourth of July celebration in Sweet, Idaho

decorated with red, white, and blue bunting. Little flags flew from the horses' bridles.

The day's activities might be held in the town square, on the main street, or in a wooded grove outside of town. Leading citizens delivered patriotic speeches and read from the Declaration of Independence. There was always a big parade led by the town band. Caught up in the spirit of the day, settlers cheered and applauded as the militia passed by. Children marched along to the beat of the fife-and-drum corps.

After the parade, the settlers would feast on their picnic lunches. Then they joined in games and sports that went on all afternoon. There were foot races, horse races, sack races and wagon races, ball games and pie-eating contests. Boys and men tried to climb greased poles or catch oiled pigs.

In the evening, fireworks lit up the sky. The day was rounded out by a community dance held on an outdoor platform by the glow of lanterns.

Many of the children who took part in these celebrations had traveled west with wagon trains. All of them had helped settle the frontier. They had faced dangers and overcome hardships that we today can only faintly imagine. It is hardly surprising that these youngsters felt proud of themselves, their communities, and their country. They would remember those Fourth of July celebrations for the rest of their lives.

Harriet Walter recalled: "How our hearts thrilled as we heard the military band which played the patriotic airs. . . . At eleven o'clock there was a parade led by the flag bearer and band. Then there was a float filled with as many little girls as we had states, little girls dressed in white with sashes and caps of red, white and blue, representing each state of the Union. In front holding the flag was the loveliest being on earth — the Goddess of Liberty — dressed in white, a silver starry crown on her head, and her long hair waving in the breeze. They sang 'America' and the 'Star Spangled Banner.' Do you wonder then that our hearts were thrilled, and that we were proud of our country, and our hearts were filled with patriotism?"

School children in Central City, Colorado

Acknowledgments

I am grateful to the following people who helped me find and select the photographs that appear in this book: William M. Roberts, The Bancroft Library, University of California; Jocelyn Moss, California Historical Society; Diane M. Rabson, Colorado Historical Society; Eleanor M. Gehres, Augie Mastrogiuseppe and Fred Yonce, Western History Department, Denver Public Library; Elizabeth Jacox, Idaho State Historical Society; Nancy Sherbert, Kansas State Historical Society; Bonnie Wilson, Minnesota Historical Society; Ouida Brown and Paul White, National Archives; John E. Carter, Nebraska State Historical Society; Jean Elkington and Susan Seyl, Oregon Historical Society; Dr. Herman Viola and Paul Fleming, Smithsonian Institution National Anthropological Archives; Kenneth W. Duckett, University of Oregon Library.

The text for this book is based on many western histories and memoirs. I am indebted to the following works in particular for special insights, details, and documentary material: *Bury My Heart at Wounded Knee: An Indian History of the American West* by Dee Brown (Holt, Rinehart & Winston, 1970); *The California Trail* by George R. Stewart (McGraw-Hill, 1962); *Far Western Frontier: 1830–1860* by Ray A. Billington (Harper & Row, 1956); *For Fear We Shall Perish* by Joseph Pigney (E. P. Dutton, 1961); *Great Documents in American Indian History* edited by Wayne

Moquin with Charles Van Doren (Praeger, 1973); *Growing Up with California* by John E. Baur (Will Kramer, 1978); *Pioneer Women: Voices from the Kansas Frontier* by Joanna L. Stratton (Simon & Schuster, 1981); *The Pioneers* by Huston Horn (Time-Life Books, 1979); *Women's Diaries of the Westward Journey* by Lillian Schlissel (Schocken Books, 1982).

The author gratefully acknowledges permission to quote from the following works:

pages 25, 26, "Female Pioneering in Oregon, 1844," manuscript diary by Martha Ann Morrison Minto. Quoted by permission of The Bancroft Library.

pages 59, 73–74, 90 and 94, *Pioneer Women: Voices from the Kansas Frontier* by Joanna L. Stratton. Copyright 1981 by Joanna L. Stratton. Reprinted by permission of Simon & Schuster, a Division of Gulf & Western Corporation.

Other quoted works are:

page 42, *Indian Boyhood* by Charles A. Eastman (McClure, Phillips, 1904).

pages 65, 71, *Prentice Mulford's Story: Or Life By Land and Sea* by Prentice Mulford (F. J. Needham, 1889).

pages 65–66, *A Backward Glance at Eighty: Recollections and Comment* by Charles A. Murdock (Paul Elder & Co., 1921).

page 83, *Adobe Days* by Sarah Bixby Smith (Jake Zeitlin, 1931).

The photographs in this book are from the following sources:

Courtesy of The Bancroft Library, University of California:
page 30.

Courtesy of the California Historical Society, San Francisco:
pages 37, 79 and 82.

Courtesy of the Colorado Historical Society:
pages 67, 76, 78 and 84.

Index

Page numbers in *italics* refer to captions.